The Way Home

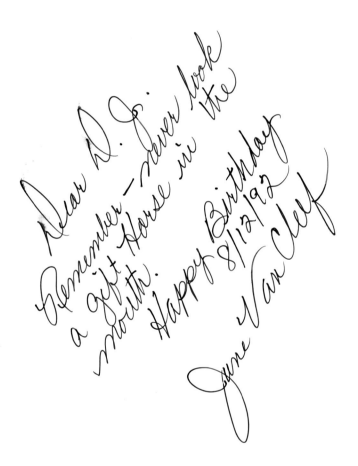

Dear D. J.:
Remember — never look
a gift Horse in the
mouth.
Happy Birthday 8/12/92
June Van Cleef

NUMBER FOUR
The Charles and Elizabeth Prothro Texas Photography Series

The Way Home

PHOTOGRAPHS FROM THE HEART OF TEXAS

By June Van Cleef

ESSAY BY BRYAN WOOLLEY

·

TEXAS A&M UNIVERSITY PRESS
College Station

The paper used in this book meets the minimum requirements
of the American National Standard for Permanence
of Paper for Printed Library Materials, Z39.48-1984.
Binding materials have been chosen for durability.

LIBRARY OF CONGRESS CATALOGING-IN-PUBLICATION DATA
Van Cleef, June, 1941–
        The way home : photographs from the heart of Texas
/ June Van Cleef ; essay by Bryan Woolley. — 1st ed.
        p.   cm. — (The Charles and Elizabeth Prothro
Texas photography series ; no. 4)
        ISBN 0-89096-444-0 (alk. paper)
        1. Hamilton County (Tex.)—Pictorial works.
2. Country life—Texas—Hamilton County—Pictorial
works.   3. Hamilton County (Tex.)—Social life and
customs—Pictorial works.   I. Woolley, Bryan.
II. Title.   III. Series.
F392.H34V36   1992
976.4'549—dc20   91-43305
                                               CIP

In memory of my father, Thomas Samuel Redford,
a loving parent and a real Texan,
and to my mother, Elta, and my daughter, Cindy,
whose love is everlasting

Contents

Preface

In 1978 I began my photography of Texas and Texans, directing my attention to rural Hamilton County in the central region of the state. It had been home to me during my high school days, but it also seemed to me that the people there were representative of rural culture elsewhere in Texas and throughout the nation. I wanted to try to capture that culture in photographs before it completely disappeared.

I wanted to know—and to show—the people who live there, to explore their attitudes and learn whether the independent frontier ethic still prevailed in some form. In their daily lives, did people still value self-reliance, industry, and individualism? Did they still love the land above all? Were they still shaped by the extremes of their environment: drought, heat, tornadic winds? My photographs show answers to such questions.

All of Texas is changing. Less than twenty percent of the state's population is rural today, and it is rapidly vanishing. Hamilton County is one of the few rural counties left in the state. Just out of reach of the sprawling populations of Dallas and Fort Worth to the northeast and of San Antonio and Austin to the south, the county specializes in livestock and grain production and in dairies. An increasing influx of hunters and other weekenders gives the residents needed income, but the town square shows the loss of regular daily trade.

In many cases in rural Texas widows carrying on the family farm and ranch businesses have become symbols of a way of life that barely hangs on but that mothered many of us who now live in cities and mourn the passing of a sense of community and of a closeness to life's processes. In the cities, closed caskets and impersonal, expensive funerals stand in stark contrast to death in rural Texas communities, where the church, mourning neighbors and family, and traditional rituals help us face our own deaths as we face the death of loved ones.

In short, I chose this photographic direction as a way home, because I love the land and the people who reside there. Rural Texas gave me birth, and I want to know it again and discover the truths that are there now. I want to find a way home, and I believe others want to, also.

Acknowledgments

I want to thank the wonderfully warm and hospitable people of the Hamilton County area who shared their lives and allowed me to photograph them. During this project, they gave me food, lodging, and wonderful memories. For this I will always be grateful.

I would especially like to thank Bill Wright of Abilene, who has been instrumental in getting funding for this photographic series and in guiding it as chair of the series committee. As a friend, he has given me encouragement and hope. Many of my friends and photography students have also given me moral and emotional support throughout this endeavor. In particular, I would like to thank Larry Range, Martha and Hubert Campbell, Cyndi Barker, and Mike Sewell.

Special thanks go to Charles and Elizabeth Prothro for the grant that made this series possible.

The Way Home

A Hamilton County Memoir

BY BRYAN WOOLLEY

They tell me of a home where my friends have gone,
O they tell me of that land far away,
Where the tree of life in eternal bloom
Sheds its fragrance thro' the unclouded day.

— HYMN

The Baptist church stood on one side of the square, and the Methodist church on the other. The Church of Christ was just across the road. In the middle of the square stood a large shed with a shingle roof. All the sides of the shed were open. Under it were rows of crude wooden benches with an aisle down the middle, and at one end of the shed was a platform for the choir and a pulpit for the evangelist. The shed was called the Tabernacle, and it was used by the churches for their revivals in the summertime.

The main purpose of the revivals was to save souls — to persuade us to desert the deadly pathways of sin, accept the Lord Jesus Christ as our personal Savior, be baptized into whichever of the households of faith was occupying the Tabernacle at the moment, and live thenceforth in the knowledge that death would not be our end, but the beginning of our eternal life of joy with God in His heaven. For those whose souls already had been saved, the revivals offered a chance to revive the spirit, to shore up a rickety determination, to suck in the gut of faith and persevere with the righteous life. And for everybody, they were a chance to get together and talk about the weather and the children and the war — World War II — in which many young men from the town and the farms were fighting, in Europe and Asia and

Africa and the South Pacific, half a world away from Carlton, Texas, and everything they had ever known.

There were two preaching services a day during the revivals—one in the morning, which was supposed to end about noon, and one in the evening.

In the evening, when the young men had finished their work for the day, and the young mothers had washed and put away the supper dishes and dressed their children in clean shirts and overalls and pinafores, and the families were arriving in the square in their old Fords and Chevrolets, there was a festive air about the revivals. Before the service, the men would lean against the cars and talk, their cigarettes glowing like orange fireflies in the darkness. The young women would hustle their babies and toddlers into the Tabernacle and arrange them along the benches, and visit with the mothers on the bench ahead and the mothers on the bench behind. We school-age kids—six to ten or so years old—would play tag or hide-and-seek among the cars until a father or mother came to herd us to the Tabernacle.

Sometimes we children would stand in front of the congregation and sing a song that we sang only at revivals:

> I've got that Baptist booster spizerinctum
> Down in my heart,
> Down in my heart,
> Down in my heart!
> I've got that Baptist booster spizerinctum
> Down in my heart,
> Down in my heart to stay!

The morning service was attended mostly by the older women and men of the town and whatever children could be dragged to it. I was about six years old when my grandmother began taking me along.

The word that comes into my mind as I remember those interminable hours of squirming on the hard wooden benches is "hot"— the perspiring faces of the women and the faint *whit, whit* of their cardboard funeral-home fans trying to stir a breeze into the sticky air; the torrid white sunlight just beyond the edge of the Tabernacle roof; the sweating evangelist, coatless, his necktie loosened, leaning over the pulpit, and his detailed description of the eternal fires of hell and the everlasting agonies of those doomed to dwell therein; the fervent tears of the repentant as they plodded down the aisle, hunched under the weight of their sins.

Outside the Tabernacle, beyond the edges of the town, under the pale, blinding sky, locusts were whirring in the creek bottoms, milk cows were grazing, and the crops that gave us our livelihood and were Carlton's only reason for being—the corn, the maize, the oats, the hay, the wheat, the cotton—were creeping silently upward from the dark earth.

One of the farms belonged to us. Our hogs were grunting in their pen, wallowing in their mud, seeking coolness. Our chickens—white Plymouth rocks and a few bantams—were strutting about the barnyard, pecking at the ground, their yellow eyes blinking. On the front porch, my father's hounds—asleep and perhaps dreaming—were thumping the floorboards with their tails. Whenever a puff of breeze came up, the windmill wheel would groan and turn a time or two, and the sucker rod would move slowly up the pipe and drop a dollop of cool water into the tank.

Except on the days when my father cranked up our old Farmall and drove it out of its shed to work the fields, and the days when my mother or my father started the car for a trip into the town, there were no noises of engines or motors on our place. The only other machinery sounds I remember were the *thunk, thunk* of the windmill sucker rod and the clatter of the old Singer sewing machine on which my mother made nearly all our clothes. It was powered by her feet on the treadle.

Pres. Franklin D. Roosevelt hadn't yet brought electricity to our house, or to any farmhouse in our part of Hamilton County. My mother washed our clothes in a big iron pot that was sitting on a wood fire in the yard. She scrubbed them on a washboard with soap homemade of lye and the fat of our butchered hog, and ironed them with heavy "sad irons" heated on the burners of her kerosene cookstove. I sounded out the words of my first-grade Dick and Jane reader by the light of the coal-oil lamp on the round oak dining table. In winter, the only heat in the house was provided by a woodstove in the living room. When my father would pile in the logs and the kindling and douse them with kerosene and throw in a match in the chilly morning, we would huddle shivering around it, holding out our hands to catch the first waves of warmth, watching the walls of the stove slowly brighten to a rosy glow. Our milk and perishables were kept in a washtub with a big block of ice on the back porch. We brought the ice from town once a week and covered the tub with an old blanket to hold in the cold. We owned a radio, but it was powered by car batteries, and our batteries were old and wouldn't hold a charge. Since the war made it impossible to buy new ones, we didn't hear the radio often. There was no telephone.

We had a cold-water faucet in the kitchen. It was the only plumbing in the house, but it was more than many of our neighbors had. We bathed in a washtub in water heated on the kitchen stove, and went to an outdoor toilet that stood some distance from the house. In the winter, our visits there were infrequent and brief, especially at night or when a norther was blowing. In the summer, copperheads sometimes would be attracted to the toilet's shade, and there were always spiders.

I was born during the Great Depression, the eldest of five. Ours wasn't the most prosperous farm in the county, but it wasn't the poorest, either. My mother says the country people didn't feel the Depression as acutely as the people in town. Being a child, I didn't feel it at all. Only years later would I learn I had been born during hard times.

We were almost self-sufficient. Our cows provided all our milk and butter. Our chickens provided our eggs and part of our meat, especially for our Sunday dinners. My mother raised a large garden. The vegetables we didn't eat fresh, she canned in Mason jars and stored in the cellar. We knocked pecans out of the trees in the creek bottoms. My father shot squirrels and rabbits and doves and quail and brought them home for us to eat. He raised most of the feed that our animals ate. Every winter, we butchered a hog, which provided not only bacon, ham, sausage, and pork chops, but lard and soap as well.

Hog-killing day was one of the days it was fun to be a child on the farm. Despite the terrible scream the animal would make as it died on that cold morning, it was a day of laughter and good feeling.

The neighbors—two or three families of them—would come. The men would kill the animal, scald its bristles off in a barrel of hot water, and butcher it. The women would salt the bacon and ham, sew the cloth sacks in which the meat would be hung in the smokehouse, grind and season the sausage, build a fire in the yard, throw the fat into my mother's iron wash pot, and render it into lard. While the fat was boiling, they would toss strips of the hog's skin into it and dip them out a few minutes later as golden, hot "cracklings," a delicacy only faintly akin to the dry, cellophaned "pork skins" sold now in supermarkets.

A lot of the work was done that way—neighbors helping each other out. The neighbors would help us butcher our hog or pick our cotton or reap and shock our oats or wheat, and we would help them with theirs. The women worked together on their canning and quilting. Everybody brought his own tools to whatever job needed doing. No money was offered or accepted among neighbors, but sometimes, when cash was needed, we would hire out to others. I remember dragging a cottonsack down the rows of Mr. Walker Bingham's field with my parents one long, hot day, and when the work was over, Mr. Bingham—one of the more well-to-do farmers of the county—gave me a shiny quarter. It was the first wages I ever was paid. I remember how hard and sharp the cotton bolls were. I remember how tired my mother was that night.

Threshing the grain was more fun than cottonpicking. My family and the neighbors would reap the crop with a horse-drawn reaper not much changed from Cyrus McCormick's original design. The machine would move around the field, cutting the plants, binding them into sheaves with twine, and spitting them onto the ground. Or was there another machine that bound the sheaves? I was very young. The rest of us would walk behind the reaper, stacking the sheaves into neat shocks. After the shocks had dried in the sun for a few days, the thresher would come.

A truck pulled the huge machine from farm to farm. Its crew came with it. The thresher, out mothers warned us every year, was dangerous, full of pulleys and gears and belts and teeth. It took special knowledge to avoid its perils and, even so, many men lost arms in threshers. Each farmer paid the owner of the thresher in cash or in a share of the crop for the services of his machine, and the owner paid his crew.

They would park the thresher in the middle of the field, and the neighbors would come with their pitchforks and help my father haul the sheaves to the thresher and the threshed grain to the barn in mule-drawn wagons, and help my mother cook the huge meal that the thresher crew and the field hands would consume under the live oak trees beside the windmill at noon.

I was too young to know it then, but the work was brutal. Having so many people on the farm — normally a lonely place — was what made the day so full of laughter.

Now all the work that was done by all those people can be done by one man on a combine. He can bring his lunch to the field with him and eat it alone in his air-conditioned cab and listen to his radio for company.

The combine and other machines — huge, costly contraptions that have replaced the brawn of humans and animals with steel and internal combustion engines and fossil fuels — are part of the reason the countryside of Hamilton County has changed so much since I lived there. It doesn't take as many heads and hands and shoulders and backs to run a farm now as it did then. Many families have lost their lands to markets and weather and banks, too. And many fields —

those where King Cotton reigned too long—are worn out and good only for grazing now.

So there are fewer farms than there used to be, and fewer farmers, and fewer neighbors. The fading remains of abandoned farm homes —leaning piles of rotting lumber, lone chimneys pointing skyward like work-worn fingers, groves of shade trees marking the homesites of long-departed families—dot the hills and prairies.

But the dwindling few who still live on the land don't have to do their laundry in the yard or read by lamplight or keep their food in washtubs or go to outdoor toilets. President Roosevelt's electric lines reached their houses long ago. They own stereos and VCRs and computers. Television comes to them by satellite. They buy most of their food in supermarkets and most of their clothing at shopping centers and discount stores, like the people in the cities. Their cars and trucks take them as far away as they want to go, and all or most of the way is paved.

Nearly all the young people ride those roads into the cities now, to schools and jobs that will divorce them from the soil forever. There's neither room nor livelihood for them anymore on the land of their ancestors.

No one who lived through the old times and has a good memory would say all the changes in the rural places are bad. Most of the people who left have no serious yearning to go back. Not to stay. Not to work there as their parents and grandparents did. Not to try to wrestle a living from the stubborn soil in the old way. To build a little weekend retreat in the country someday, maybe. To go hunting or fishing. To try to find old landmarks that still live in memory. To visit the graves of their forebears.

I don't know how long ago my ancestors—the DeVolins, the Gibsons, the Whites, the Woolleys—settled in Hamilton County. Some of them, I know, moved there while the Comanches still roamed the land. All my great-grandparents and grandparents but one—my maternal grandmother, Clora DeVolin Gibson—are buried there. But

no living member of any of my ancestral families is in the county now.

There are thousands of families like us from many parts of rural America. Our exodus from the countryside happened all of a sudden, during the life span of a single, still-not-old generation — we who were the children in the Tabernacle during the great war that changed everything. And as our land has emptied, the little towns that lived to serve us have shriveled.

The Way Home

The Carlton of my childhood had a cotton gin and a feed mill, two grocery stores, a blacksmith shop, three gas stations, a laundry, a feed store, a barber shop, a Masonic lodge, a beauty shop, a telephone office, a variety store, a post office, a doctor, and a drugstore. On a hill on the edge of the town stood the two-story stone schoolhouse where I went to first grade and my grandmother Gibson taught for many years. My great-grandfather's name—I. J. Gibson—was on the cornerstone.

But the school is shut down now. Its last class graduated in 1969. Of downtown Carlton, only one business—the grocery store that belonged to Hob Thompson—survives. The Tabernacle no longer stands amidst the churches. One of the churches—the Methodist—is dead. The others are fading shadows of the robust congregations they used to be. Their *spizerinctum* is gone. If the Tabernacle still stood, and if there were to be a revival, no mothers with babies would be there, and no children playing hide-and-seek among the cars. No young sinners would be moving down the aisle toward their salvation.

Only a few dozen people remain in the town that used to be home to hundreds. Nearly all of them are old. As they depart, their places won't be filled by newcomers or new generations. Soon Carlton—like Sunshine and Honey Grove and Fairy and Aleman and the other rural communities that time already has wiped from Hamilton County— will live only in the memories of a few old people, and then they'll die, too.

In 1986, the sesquicentennial year of the Republic of Texas, the remaining citizens of Carlton collected the memories of many families who used to live there and in the countryside around, and compiled them into a book. In it, Betty Jo Fine McKenney, a woman of my mother's generation, wrote of her grandson, who lives in a city: "I have taken him to Carlton and shown him the names on the graves at the cemetery and explained to him how it was at one time, in the hope that we can pass it on to another generation."

My own sons were born in 1969 and 1971. They've always lived in cities. One day when they were small, I was telling them some of the things that I've told here, and one of them said, "You sound like you lived in pioneer days." To children born after men had walked on the moon, boys who flew in airplanes when they were infants and studied computers along with their spelling and multiplication tables, these memories *are* of "pioneer days"—a time when Texas and America were younger, fresher, simpler, and less crowded than they are now. Even so, those days aren't yet past memory, and the bitter words of the Old Testament's Preacher needn't be let to come true: "There is no remembrance of former things, nor will there be any remembrance of later things yet to happen among those who come after."

Those who come after should at least hear the echoes and see the shadows.

The Plates

Their small living room was filled with photographs of their children, grandchildren, and great-grandchildren. Among the fading color images I spotted a black and white photograph of a young couple. "Oh, that's Amos and me when we were first married," Mrs. French chuckled. "I was only sixteen." Amos added, "When we first married, we sharecropped around in Hamilton County. Didn't make any money, though, until we started farming thirds and two-thirds."

PLATE 1
"Amos and Ethelene French," 1988
Hamilton County
Silver Gelatin print

14

My Sister, Nancy

In the late afternoon light I stopped to watch a cocky young cowboy shoeing his horse. "This ol' paint turned out to be my best horse," Ricky Fuqua said. "He's stubborn but he's tough and can hold up through a full day of hard cow workin'."

PLATE 3
"Ricky Fuqua," 1988
Hamilton County
Silver Gelatin Print

18

One day, quite by surprise, I received a dozen yellow roses from my father. I drove two hundred miles to photograph him holding those roses. When I arrived, he was working cattle.

PLATE 5
"He Sent Roses," 1981
Hamilton County
Palladium Composite Print

The rattlers, worn as a trophy from the annual rattlesnake hunt, were artfully attached to this young man's handmade leather hatband. The act of wearing them gave him distinction among his peers.

For my brother, Sam, the oil lamps are a reminder of his childhood days growing up on a large West Texas ranch miles from the nearest electrical power.

PLATE 7
"Sam Redford," 1979
Hamilton County
Silver Gelatin Print

26

"Jessica was the best cattle dog I ever had," Tom said.

"Do you like wild Mustang grape cobbler? I fixed some for us to eat after we finish working cattle." With these words, Frances Gardner welcomed me to her ranch and to a full day of ranch work. Like many other Texas ranchwomen, Frances runs a business, does most of the ranch work, and still makes a tasty cobbler.

PLATE 9
"Frances Gardner," 1988
Hamilton County
Silver Gelatin Print

He proudly exhibited on his walls photographs of his pioneer father. "In the end," Bart Oates said, "what matters most to a man is to have the love, affection, and understanding of his family."

The sound of cattle bawling and the auctioneer calling, the smell of manure and cigars blended together. Occasionally one man would raise his hand to place a bid.

Like her grandfather, Edd Black, Monica is a natural with her horse — climbing all over him without the least bit of fear. Her grandfather has purchased a place every ten years, and in his will he has stipulated that his children cannot sell the property or borrow money against it. He wants the land to stay in the family and go to his grandchildren.

The strength to "stick it out"— it both preserves and destroys, as most ranchers and farmers know.

PLATE 14
"T. S. Redford," 1982
Lund Ranch, Hamilton County
Silver Gelatin Print

In the midst of working cattle, my father paused to button the pocket on his chaps. His hand is scarred from years of working to preserve and maintain the livestock, the family, and the land. It is a gentle, caring hand, yet also hard and rigid, struggling to hold up against time, drought, and all the elements that trespass on life.

PLATE 15
"Portrait of a Hand," 1982
Hamilton County
Silver Gelatin Print

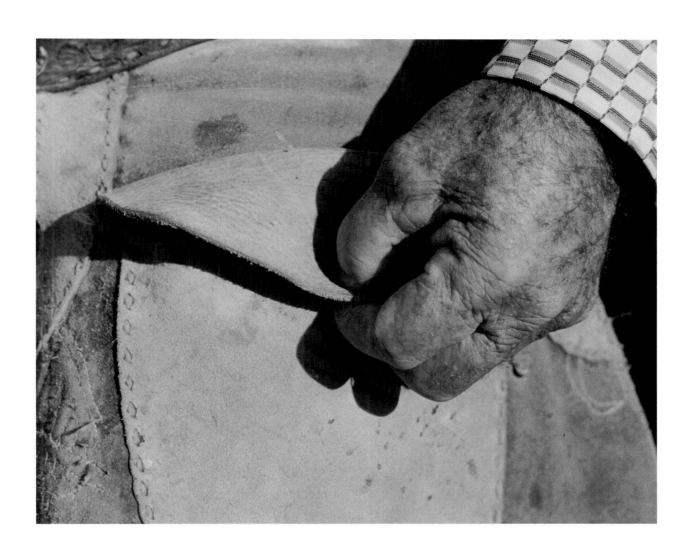

PLATE 16
"Jimmy Chumney and Fellow Cowboys," 1984
Johnny Harris Ranch, Hamilton County
Silver Gelatin Print

In a small cafe in Evant I saw an old acquaintance, Jimmy Chumney, whom I had photographed four years before. He was enjoying his favorite meal: chicken fried steak, mashed potatoes, cream gravy, and biscuits. Between big bites of steaming hot food, he talked about the days of working on ranches and breaking horses. The demand for a cowboy's services was no longer enough to keep a man going, he told me, "so I went to work for the sheriff's department in Coryell County —the pay is steady. I miss cowboying, though."

PLATE 17
"Jimmy Chumney," 1988
Hamilton County, near Evant
Silver Gelatin Print

"When my wife and I die, we want to be buried on that hill over yonder so we can look down here and see that the cows are being milked every morning and evening," Edd Black said.

PLATE 18
"Edd Black," 1988
Hico
Silver Gelatin Print

48

Carlton was a lively town several decades ago, with a busy cotton gin, a bank, stores, filling stations, several churches, a school, and a railroad. The old-timers still tell of a killing that took place on Main Street one Christmas in the 1930s. It was snowing when the town's deputy sheriff, Audie Gibson, was called to the scene of a robbery. The two burglars shot him and left him to die in the snow. When I took this picture in 1988, only the post office, one grocery store, a domino hall, and two churches remained open.

PLATE 19
"Carlton Main Street," 1988
Carlton, Hamilton County
Silver Gelatin Print

Gordon Thames was in the Carlton Grocery Store stocking up on Skoal when I stepped inside. He greeted me, "Lady, are you lost or something?" It was a weekday morning, and the store was busy with people buying a few groceries, having a soft drink, and catching up on the local news. According to Carolyn Cook, the owner, the major function of her store is that of an information center. People come to find out who is in the hospital or who has had company over the weekend.

I asked an old-timer about the house on the hill near the closed school. In the early forties, he told me, the Carlton schoolteacher, Mrs. Gibson, had lived there. The house had been locked and boarded up since she moved away many years ago.

PLATE 21
"Deserted House," 1988
Carlton
Silver Gelatin Print

54

Built in 1917, the Carlton Baptist Church appeared almost unchanged by time. The Sunday I was there the opened windows allowed the hot August breeze to fill the building. The sounds of creaking fans as they turned, the occasional squeak of a chair being moved, and men's voices as they discussed Christ in their lives all blended rhythmically together to form an ancient sort of music.

PLATE 22
"Men's Sunday School Class," 1988
Bob Southerland, Jerry Cole, and Virgil Battershell
Carlton
Silver Gelatin Print

56

"Go forth and spread the word of the Lord!" the Rev. David Keith admonished at the end of the Sunday service.

"I tried to get people here interested in starting a museum to attract tourists and bring in money, but they don't want people coming here and they don't care about a museum, so I'm closing up this old drugstore and just going to enjoy it myself," said Bob Hefner. "I could sell my old-fashioned fountain and get out of debt, but I had rather have it than the money—it gives me pleasure."

PLATE 24
"Hico Drugstore Interior," 1988
Hico
Silver Gelatin Print

"Americans should own America. Foreign ownership of this country is the beginning of the end," Ronnie Wenzel said as he stood beside the sausages he makes and sells at his local business. His nickname, The Dutchman, bespeaks his own family's German (Deutsche) origins.

"We would do without most anything in order to continue to live here. The land, our horses and llamas, and our other animals mean more to us than expensive cars and fine clothes ever could." Like a growing number of other rural Texans, Amye and Ken Craig have turned to raising exotics to help keep their place going.

PLATE 28
"Johnny Slough, Deputy Sheriff," 1988
Hamilton
Silver Gelatin Print

Louella Lightfoot probably can get tough, but she seems to be more of a mother figure than a jailer to most of the prisoners, especially the younger ones. A young man occupied number two; he had been arrested for going berserk and shooting up the family homeplace. Louella talked to him like a son, "Honey, put your shirt on, and what about your hair?"

Roy Chumney, talking about being a native of the area, jokingly told this story. An old-timer was sitting peacefully under the Tree of Knowledge in front of the courthouse discussing what it took to be a "true Hamiltonian." "Well," he drawled, "first, both you and your father before you must have been born in the county and, second, you need to be a Protestant and preferably a Baptist."

Growing up in a small West Texas town, we children sometimes played on the courthouse lawn and would occasionally tiptoe inside to enter what seemed like a mysterious world of very serious adults. Entering the Hamilton County Courthouse, I again felt that sense of exploration — stark hallways and high ceilings, women working among valuable records in rooms with vaulted doors, and bulletin boards filled with important notices.

PLATE 31
"La Juan Mizell, District Clerk," 1981
Hamilton
Silver Gelatin Print

Betty Jenkins, self-assured and possessing a hearty laugh, was Hamilton's first and only female county judge. We sat in her courtroom and talked about her years as a public official.

The plaque on the wall over his typewriter read, "Humor is the best sense we all have in common." Bob Miller's humor about local people and events, printed in his weekly column in the *Hamilton Herald-News* from 1965 until his retirement in 1983, was part of how he tried to serve his community.

PLATE 33
"Bob Miller, Publisher," 1988
Hamilton
Silver Gelatin Print

For more than fifty years Guffey Barkley made the early-morning trip from his home to the Hamilton National Bank to open it for daily business.

"Mom and Pop" Jordan's drugstore on the square was the hub of teen-
age activity in the forties, fifties, and sixties. The town youth met here
for lunch and after school for a "milk drink" or root beer. "Things
have changed," Mom told me. The teenagers prefer to ride around
in their cars and listen to loud radios. They meet at drive-ins on the
outskirts of town. Jordan's is now a pharmacy and not the drugstore
of yesterday.

PLATE 35
"Mom and Pop's Drugstore," 1988
Hamilton
Silver Gelatin Print

When I was in high school in the fifties, times were difficult. Hamilton County was in the middle of a drought, and there seemed to be no money in the town and few jobs for teenagers. I remember walking around the square, going into each business and trying to get work. When I came to the Haskell Harelik Dry Goods Store, I swallowed hard and went inside to ask Milton Harelik for work. He smiled. "Aren't you an artist who has painted several murals? I need an autumn scene to use in my store window."

PLATE 36
"Milton Harelik," 1988
Hamilton
Silver Gelatin Print

84

The Communion service at historic St. Mary's Episcopal Church had begun, and Shana George served as acolyte. She had such calmness and ritualistic demeanor.

"Untouched is the essence of Hamilton County," said June Miller Mc-Clung. "It is untouched by urbanization and industrialization, and that, along with my love for the family farmland, is why I came back home."

"I can't imagine anyone wanting to do just one thing for an entire lifetime." After having several careers and living in numerous interesting places, Catherine Randolph returned home.

PLATE 39
"Catherine Randolph," 1988
Hamilton
Silver Gelatin Print

90

Joan Crumrine had just finished a watercolor painting of flowers when I photographed her. She told me a story from her childhood: the little girl had walked along her grandfather's couch, drawing on the wall behind it. She created a scene of people in a long procession — walking, riding horseback, driving funny cars — on their way to church. At the end of the couch she drew a beautiful church with arched windows and a tall belfry. Her grandfather, elated over such a display of talent, placed a frame around the drawing. She, the child, had created a drawing; her grandfather's pride created an artist.

I followed Charlie Murphree through her beautiful family home, listening as she talked about her years growing up in it. On her wedding day many years ago, she had descended these stairs to be married in the adjoining parlor.

PLATE 41
"Charlie Murphree," 1981
Hamilton
Silver Gelatin Print

94

Ann Alexander, a descendant of early settlers in the area, with her husband and later her son ran one of the few industries in the county, Alexander Molding Mill, one of the largest plants of its kind in the state. Ann was proud that the employment their mill offered area residents helped keep some of the young people from moving away to nearby cities.

PLATE 42
"Ann Alexander," 1988
Hamilton
Silver Gelatin Print

96

"I am trying to sell this house," said Erna Ruth Campbell as she and her son Drew met me at the door. "Now that Andy is gone, I want to get a new start. This house holds too many memories."

PLATE 43
"The Campbells," 1988
Hamilton
Silver Gelatin Print

98

Most small Texas communities have a domino hall on the town square, but this was my first visit inside one. Gaining admittance wasn't easy. The domino players told me I was the first woman in their recollection to be allowed inside.

PLATE 44
"Domino Hall," 1981
Hamilton
Silver Gelatin Print

100

Amos French farmed for years. When I visited with him, he still had a few cattle and plowed a small field, but he spent most of his time playing dominoes. "I don't usually play dominoes in town," he said, "because you can't talk and I like to talk when I play. In town they tap out their scores so as not to speak a word out loud. That's too serious for me."

The first rural woman I knew, my mother, has always been there—giving, caring, providing. Some rural women in Texas continue in traditional roles, and many run the homesteads alone. Others work in their own careers and help keep the farms and ranches solvent.

PLATE 46
"Elta Redford," 1981
Hamilton County
Palladium Print

104

Northwest of Pottsville the land becomes barren and rocky, and the only trees are mesquite. It is definitely sheep and goat country, and Milton Stegemoller, whose face told of his many years of ranching, had raised goats most of his life. "There aren't many natives left here anymore," Milton drawled, "and those who stayed, stayed too long and now are too poor to get out. So they just stay some more."

PLATE 47
"Milton Stegemoller," 1988
Pottsville Community, Hamilton County
Silver Gelatin Print

There were some black sheep—and goats—in the Adams herd, and that was just the way Henny wanted it. She and J. W. had lived in the rocky hills of the south part of the county for the past thirty years, raising superior registered Angora goats and Katahdin sheep. "To excel is in my blood," Henny told me. "My maiden name is Case, and my father was the originator of Case tractors. He believed in producing the best."

Henny Adams spins her own yarn from the wool she and her husband produce. She uses natural colors of cream white, brown, and warm black to weave her original pieces.

PLATE 49
"Henny Adams," 1988
Hamilton County
Silver Gelatin Print

110

Tall prairie grasses once swayed in the breeze on this land. The early settlers burned the grasses and overgrazed the land, first with cattle and then with sheep. The farmers cut the land with their plows and, in some cases, left it depleted of its former richness. The tall native grasses disappeared forever.

PLATE 50
"Plowed Land," 1988
Hamilton County
Silver Gelatin Print

112

"Dadburn it! This is probably the last year Smith & Jones will be ginning," exclaimed Ollie Zschiesche, who had worked at this cotton gin since 1947. No reporter came to hail the end of the cotton era in the county; its passing was quiet and unnoticed by most.

PLATE 51
"Ollie Zschiesche," 1988
Hamilton
Silver Gelatin Print

114

"You're seeing the end of it. This is the last year I will plant cotton."
As Lloyd Melde talked, he crumbled a dried cotton leaf in his hand
and let the wind carry it away. His father, William Melde, had paid
for the family farm with cotton, but the time when a man could do
that had passed. As I left, Lloyd said resignedly, "My family is tired."

I had never met Oleta Stegemoller before, but when I told her I was photographing people of rural Texas, she invited me in for a cup of tea. When she and her husband, Oscar, were first married, she said, they had a team of horses named Doll and Blue. Sometimes when Oscar was hauling corn from the fields, the wagon would veer too far to the right or the left. Oscar would say, "Blue, move over to the left," and she would, or "Doll, move to the right" and she would. Oscar died in 1985 of Rocky Mountain spotted fever, but Oleta's conversation still centered on him.

PLATE 53
"Oleta Stegemoller," 1988
Pottsville Community
Silver Gelatin Print

I was among those who attended the funeral service of Bruno Schneider, a long-time friend and neighbor of my parents. Outside the hundred-year-old St. Paul's Lutheran Church the milo was swaying in the hot July breeze, and the humming of the locusts blended with the music. After the service, as has been the custom for generations, the people walked in procession from the church to the burial site.

PLATE 54
"Bruno Schneider's Funeral—Arriving," 1988
Monroe Streger, Werner Schrank, and Henry Wenzel
St. Paul's Lutheran Church
Aleman Community
Silver Gelatin Print

PLATE 56
"Bruno Schneider's Funeral—Mourners," 1988
Herman Wenzel and Melvin and Peggy Wenzel
St. Paul's Lutheran Church
Aleman Community
Silver Gelatin Print

124

PLATE 58
"Bruno Schneider's Funeral—Procession," 1988
Pastors Edward Schneider and John Feierabend Lead the Procession
St. Paul's Lutheran Church
Aleman Community
Silver Gelatin Print

128

At sunset Mary Schneider returned to the graveyard. As we talked, she bent down and picked up a red carnation that one of the pall-bearers had worn. "I'm going to keep running the place and raising cattle," she said. "I've done it before by myself and I'll do it again."

In 1917, when the first Bosse arrived in Shive and opened a blacksmith shop, the town was a busy farming community. He spent his days repairing wagons, shoeing horses and mules, and sharpening plow blades. Today, the Bosse Garage and Body Shop is the only business open in Shive. The sons, Edwin and Leslie, and one grandson, Mike, are the owners and the workers, repairing cars, pickups, and all types of farming equipment.

PLATE 60
"Bosse Garage," 1988
Leslie Bosse with Edwin and Mike in Background
Shive Community, Hamilton County
Silver Gelatin Print

132

"My mother had just finished a quilt the day before she died. She was ninety-seven," Clara Landua told me when I came to get the beautiful Lone Star quilt. The top had been pieced by my Grandmother Luedecke many years before, and Clara quilted it in the summer of 1988.

Kill a hog, make sausage, and have a Schrank family reunion.

The Schrank and Gromatzky reunion is probably one of the largest family gatherings in any county of Texas, with some three hundred family members in attendance each year. The family's patriarch and his wife, August and Julie Schrank, arrived in Texas in 1853, and several generations later their descendants still hold to many of their German customs. At their 1988 reunion, the food, music, and dancing expressed a blending of cultures. Werner Schrank played songs like "Waltz across Texas" and "Fraulein" on the accordion.

PLATE 63
"Schrank-Gromatzky Family Reunion," 1988
Martin Schrank's Farm
Aleman Community
Silver Gelatin Print

Other family members danced to country and western music and ate barbecued cabrito and German sausage.

PLATE 64
"Michael Schrank Dances," 1988
Schrank-Gromatzky Family Reunion
Martin Schrank's Farm
Aleman Community
Silver Gelatin Print

140

A descendant of August and Julie Schrank, Allison Garrick.

He wore his Sunday hat and his best boots to honor the important occasion. My parents were celebrating fifty years of marriage.

Seeing her young face free of make-up, her hair in braids, her hands stained with blackberries, I supposed she would marry a local boy, remain in rural Texas, and be content with the simple life. No, she said: I will live in a big city, make lots of money, have an expensive car, and work in an office on the fifteenth floor of a high-rise business building.

PLATE 67
"Sandra Redford Picking Blackberries," 1980
Hamilton County
Silver Gelatin Print

A sense of place is created from the items of everyday life—boxes of fresh onions on the porch floor, buckets of peppers from the summer garden, muddy boots and shoes placed neatly in a cardboard box, hats hanging from steer horns, and a home-painted rural scene.

My daughter, Cindy, learned country ways and learned to love the land. Fewer and fewer do.

PLATE 69
"Cindy," 1979
Hamilton County
Silver Gelatin Print

150

Cindy and her husband, Mark, came from strong roots. Like many rural-based young people they could look forward together to a good life. She is still my Sunshine Girl.

The Way Home was composed into type on a Compugraphic digital phototypesetter in twelve point Garamond with three points of spacing between the lines. Garamond was also selected for display. The book was designed by Jim Billingsley, typeset by Metricomp, Inc., printed offset by Hart Graphics, Inc., and bound by John H. Dekker & Sons, Inc. The paper on which this book is printed carries acid-free characteristics for an effective life of at least three hundred years.

TEXAS A&M UNIVERSITY PRESS
College Station